# Rig it Right
Essentials

# West Coast SPORT FISH

I0809649

# CONTENTS

**Rigs Salmon** **4**

Delta Diver & Salmon Bungee 4

Delta Diver & Spinner Rig 5

Spin-N-Glo Rig 5

Basic Plunking Rig 6

Deepwater Bobber Float Rig 7

Anchored Boat Rig 8

Back Bouncing Plugs 9

Basic Prawn Trolling Rig 10

**Rigs Salmon - ID and Fishing Techniques** **10**

Chinook Salmon 10

Sockeye Salmon 11

Chum Salmon 11

Coho Salmon 11

**Rigs Steelhead** **12**

Pencil Lead Cinch 12

Double Hook Side - Drifting Rig And Slinky 13

Float Fishing Rigs 14

Spawn Sac Rig 16

Diver and Bait Rigs 16

Pink Plastic Worm Rig 17

Side-Planer Rigs 18

**Rigs Steelhead - ID and Fishing Techniques** **19**

Steelhead 19

**Rigs Trout and Kokanee Rigs** **20**
Trolling Rig 20
Bottom Rig 21
Float Rigs 22
Down Rigger Setups 24
**Rigs Trout and Kokanee Rigs - ID and Fishing Techniques** **25**
Bull Trout 25
Kokanee 25
Brown Trout 25
Lake Trout 26
Rainbow Trout 26
**Rigging Natural Live Baits** **27**
Frog 27
Crickets and Grasshoppers 28
Crawdads 28
Nightcrawlers 29
Caterpillars and Smaller Grubs 30
Minnows 30

# RIGS Salmon

## Ocean, Estuary and Bay Trolling Rigs

## DELTA DIVER & SALMON BUNGEE

Attach Delta Diver to leader clip

4 to 6 feet,
25 to 50 pound leader

Salmon Bungee

Silver Horde Lou Pack Wobbler

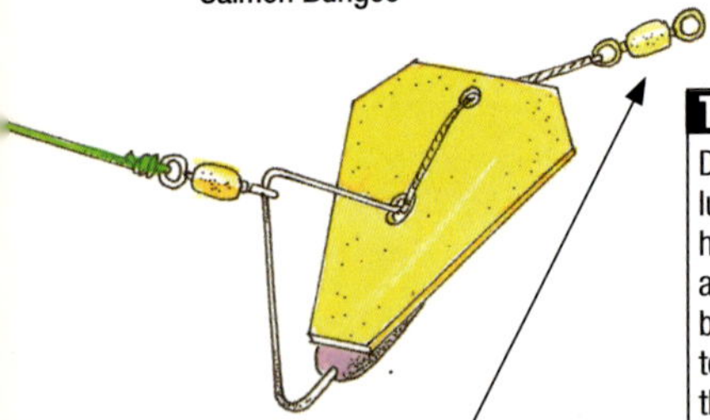

Attach Delta Driver to clip

### TIP

Delta Divers are a great way of keeping lures in the strike zone and are a must-have in any salmon anglers trolling arsenal, while a Salmon Bungee between the diver and lure allows fish to take the lure and effectively hook themselves without snapping the rig. There are a wide variety of wobblers, spoons and spinners available for use on this rig setup.

# DELTA DIVER & SPINNER RIG

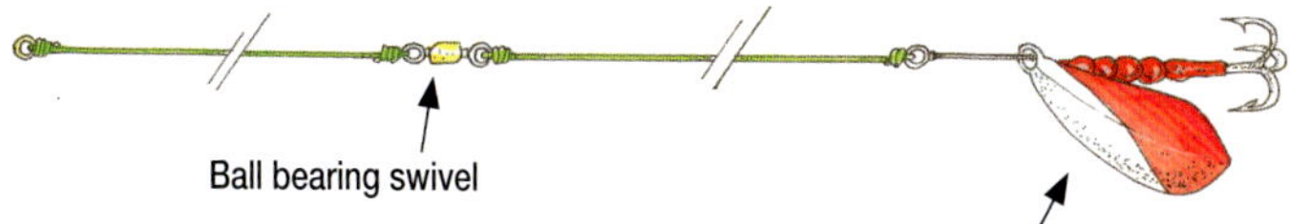


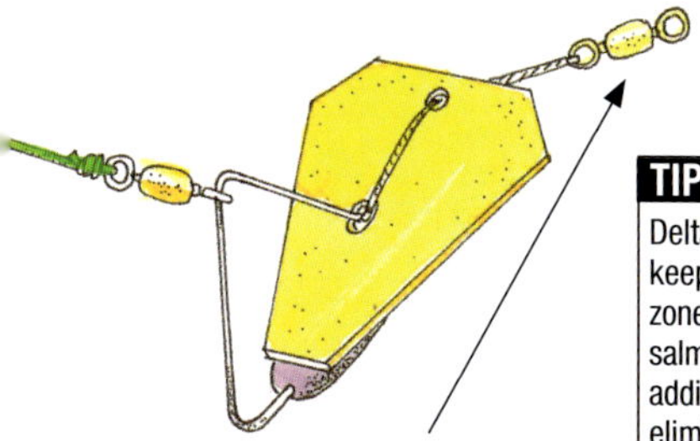


**TIP**

Delta Divers are a great way of keeping baits in the strike zone and are a must-have in any salmon anglers trolling arsenal. The addition of a ball-bearing swivel helps eliminate line twists when using spinners.

# SPIN-N-GLO RIG

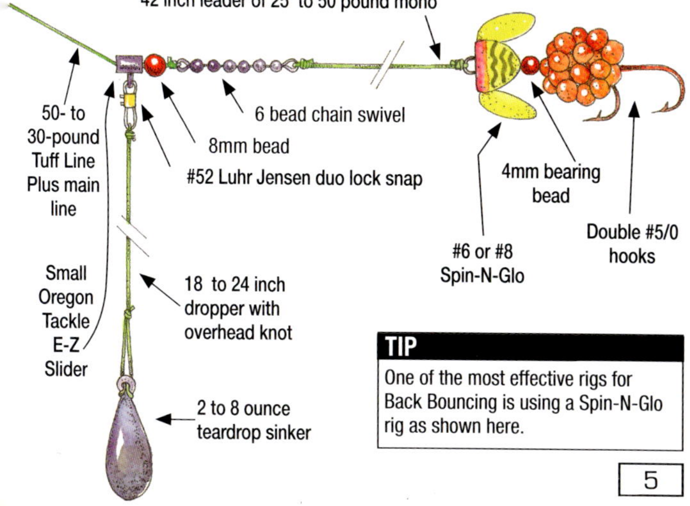


**TIP**

One of the most effective rigs for Back Bouncing is using a Spin-N-Glo rig as shown here.

# BASIC PLUNKING RIG

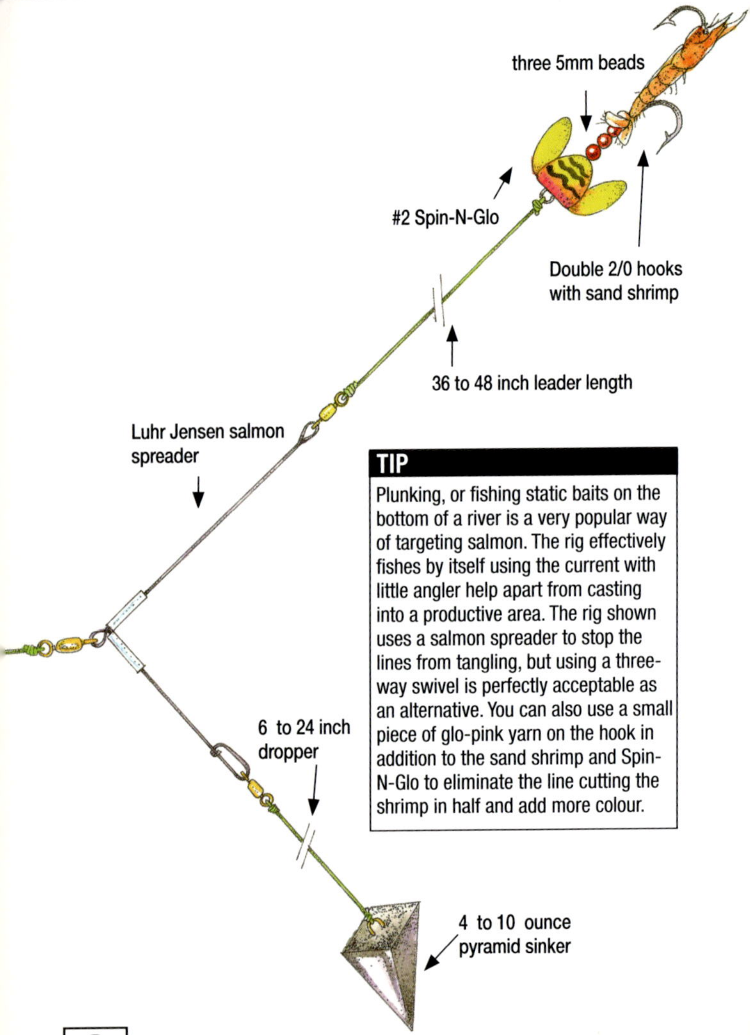


**TIP**

Plunking, or fishing static baits on the bottom of a river is a very popular way of targeting salmon. The rig effectively fishes by itself using the current with little angler help apart from casting into a productive area. The rig shown uses a salmon spreader to stop the lines from tangling, but using a three-way swivel is perfectly acceptable as an alternative. You can also use a small piece of glo-pink yarn on the hook in addition to the sand shrimp and Spin-N-Glo to eliminate the line cutting the shrimp in half and add more colour.

# DEEPWATER BOBBER FLOAT RIG

## TIP

Fishing bobbers to salmon is great fun. It's important to always keep your bait down near the bottom where the fish are holding. This rig is for deep, fast water hence the heavy lead ball. When fishing low, quieter water you can simply replace the bobber and the weight with lighter versions. It's also effective using jigs weighing from ¼ to ½ an ounce with a swivel up the line instead of a weight, or a bright pink plastic worm underneath a swivel weight.

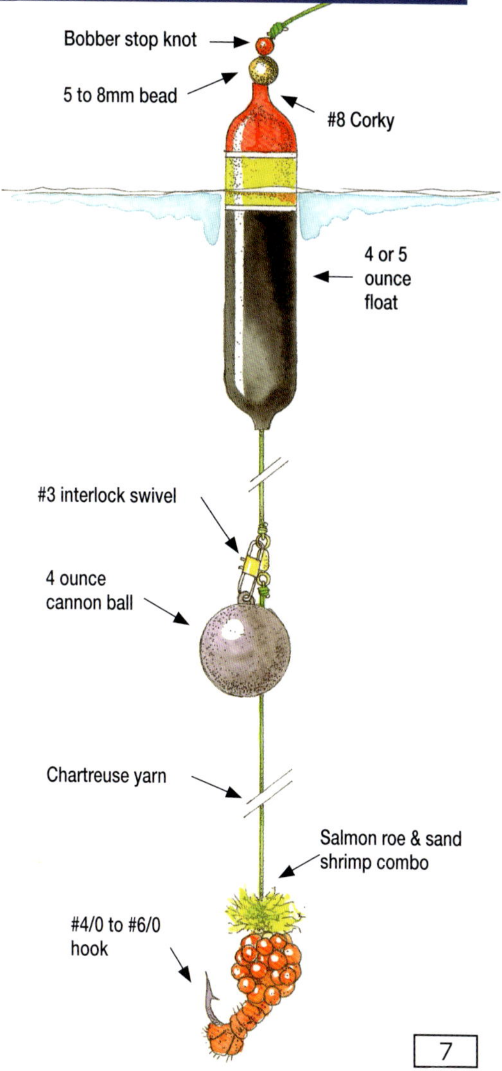

# ANCHORED BOAT RIG

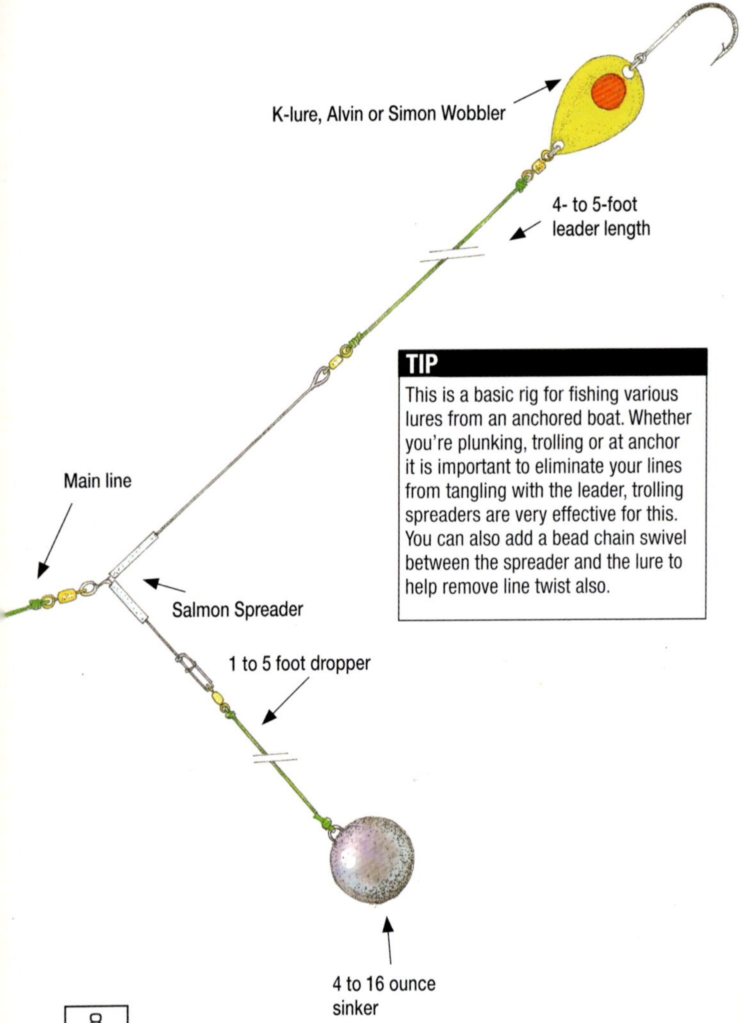


## TIP

This is a basic rig for fishing various lures from an anchored boat. Whether you're plunking, trolling or at anchor it is important to eliminate your lines from tangling with the leader, trolling spreaders are very effective for this. You can also add a bead chain swivel between the spreader and the lure to help remove line twist also.

# BACK BOUNCING PLUGS

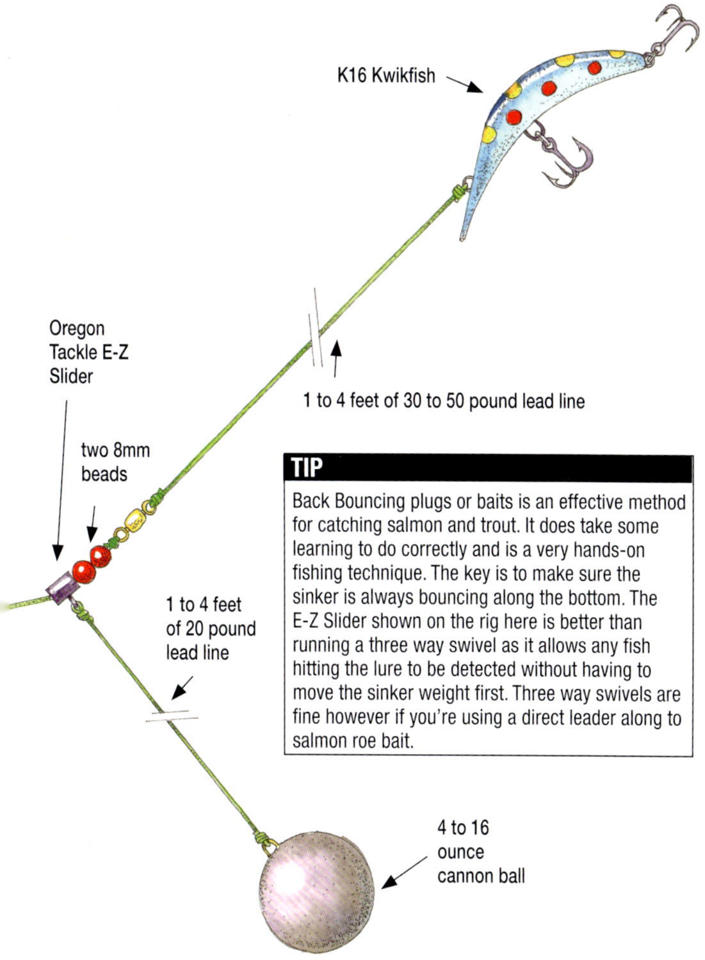


## TIP

Back Bouncing plugs or baits is an effective method for catching salmon and trout. It does take some learning to do correctly and is a very hands-on fishing technique. The key is to make sure the sinker is always bouncing along the bottom. The E-Z Slider shown on the rig here is better than running a three way swivel as it allows any fish hitting the lure to be detected without having to move the sinker weight first. Three way swivels are fine however if you're using a direct leader along to salmon roe bait.

# BASIC PRAWN TROLLING RIG

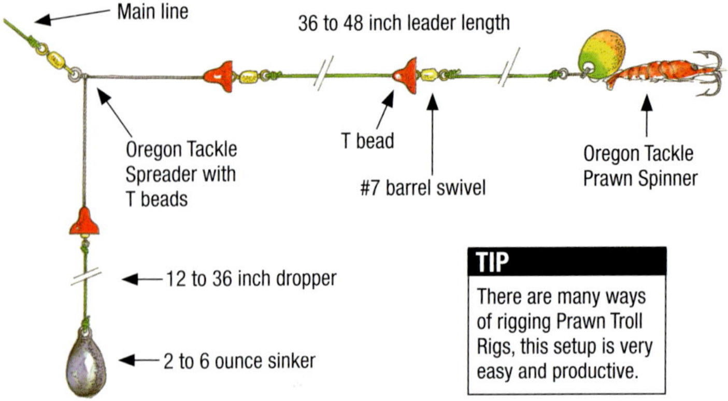


**TIP**

There are many ways of rigging Prawn Troll Rigs, this setup is very easy and productive.

# CHINOOK SALMON

A mighty and strong fighting fish, deserving of the name 'king'. Most Pacific anglers concentrate their efforts on catching these fish when they enter bays and estuaries on the spawning runs. Strong spin, baitcast and light saltwater tackle are employed, often trolling deep plugs and spoons, or live and dead fish baits behind flashers and dodgers to attract the fish's attention.

Casting lures such as spoons and spinners, and streamer or egg pattern flies in stream mouths and further upstream is effective.

# SOCKEYE SALMON

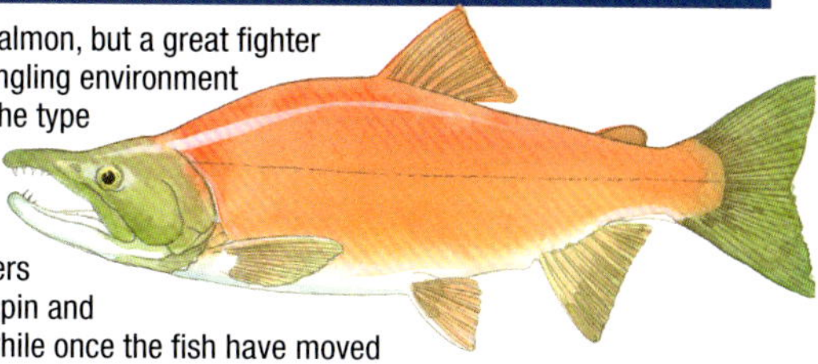

Not the best of the salmon, but a great fighter none the less. The angling environment usually determines the type and strength of tackle being used. In estuaries and big brawling rivers anglers tend to use stouter spin and baitcasting tackle, while once the fish have moved further upriver, lighter spin and fly tackle come into their own. Once they have moved upstream to spawn they stop feeding and anglers need to elicit aggressive territorial strikes.

Before the fish run upriver, they are trolled for in the estuaries and large downstream river mouths down deep with large flies and flashy lures.

# CHUM SALMON

A solid fighting fish when taken early on during their spawning aggregation. Once they start to turn color they start to deteriorate. Usually targeted on spin or fly tackle. Small spoons and spinners work well for lure anglers, while fly anglers prefer streamer flies and shrimp patterns.

# COHO SALMON

A great fighting fish that leaps and performs strong speedy runs when hooked. Mostly targeted trolling deep with heavy rods and large spoons, plugs and rigged live baitfish or fillets. They will hit cast lures and flies on lighter tackle when they are within reach and near the surface in bays, estuaries and rivers. They like flashy metallic spinners and streamer flies.

They are also targeted by angler's drift fishing and using live or dead baitfish.

## PENCIL LEAD CINCH

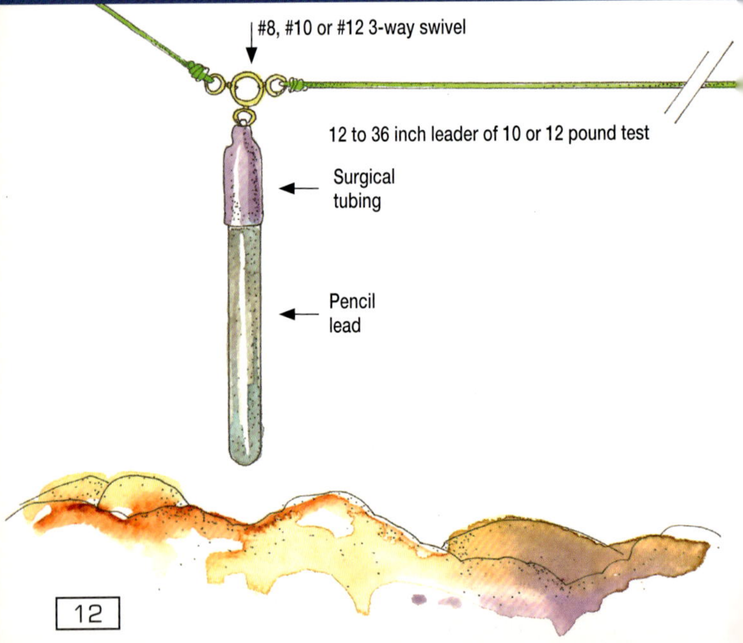

# DOUBLE HOOK SIDE-DRIFTING RIG AND SLINKY

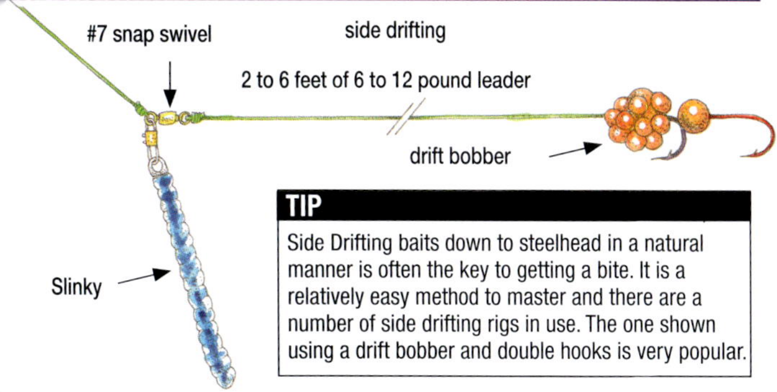


**TIP**

Side Drifting baits down to steelhead in a natural manner is often the key to getting a bite. It is a relatively easy method to master and there are a number of side drifting rigs in use. The one shown using a drift bobber and double hooks is very popular.

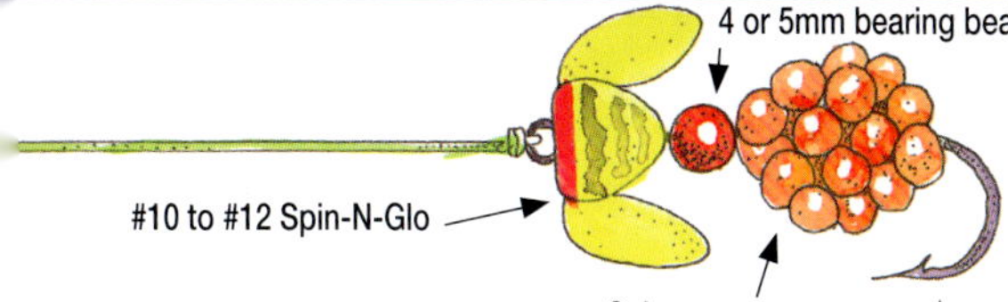


**TIP**

There are many ways to add weight in front of a Spin-N-Glo, Glo Bug yarn or Spawn Sac etc. A pencil lead, hollow core or solid is one of the most effective, economical and easy to use. Solid pencil lead is best attached to your line using a Lead Cinch that consists or a three-way swivel and length of surgical tubing into which the pencil lead is inserted.

# FLOAT FISHING RIGS

## TIP

There's probably nothing more natural for many anglers than fishing a float (bobber) rig. There are a variety of baits that can be used as well as rigging setups. But possibly the best setup is to utilize a slip bobber setup instead of a fixed float rig. Slip bobber rigs are easier to cast. There are many different bobbers available as well as a variety of baits and lures to entice both salmon and steelhead. Some popular choices of baits include jigs, salmon row, plastic worms and sand shrimp.

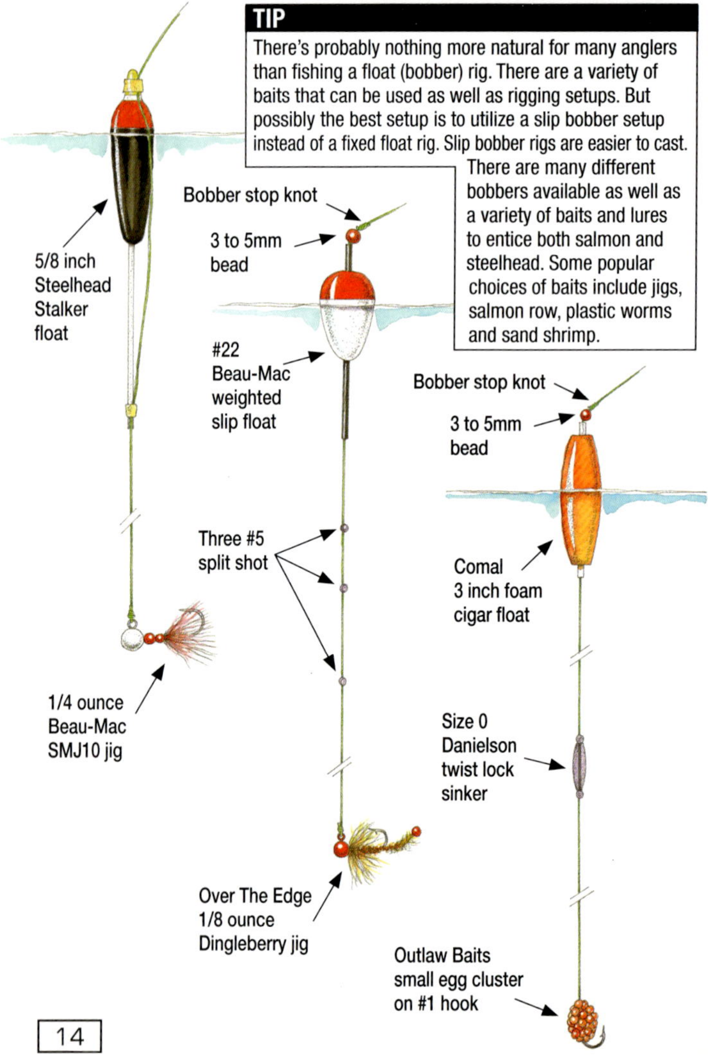

## TIP

For anglers just getting into steelheading, a basic float and worm, or float and jighead is simple to rig and very effective and deadly. Fish the rigs dead drift with the current and set the worm or baits so that they drift roughly 12 inches off the bottom.

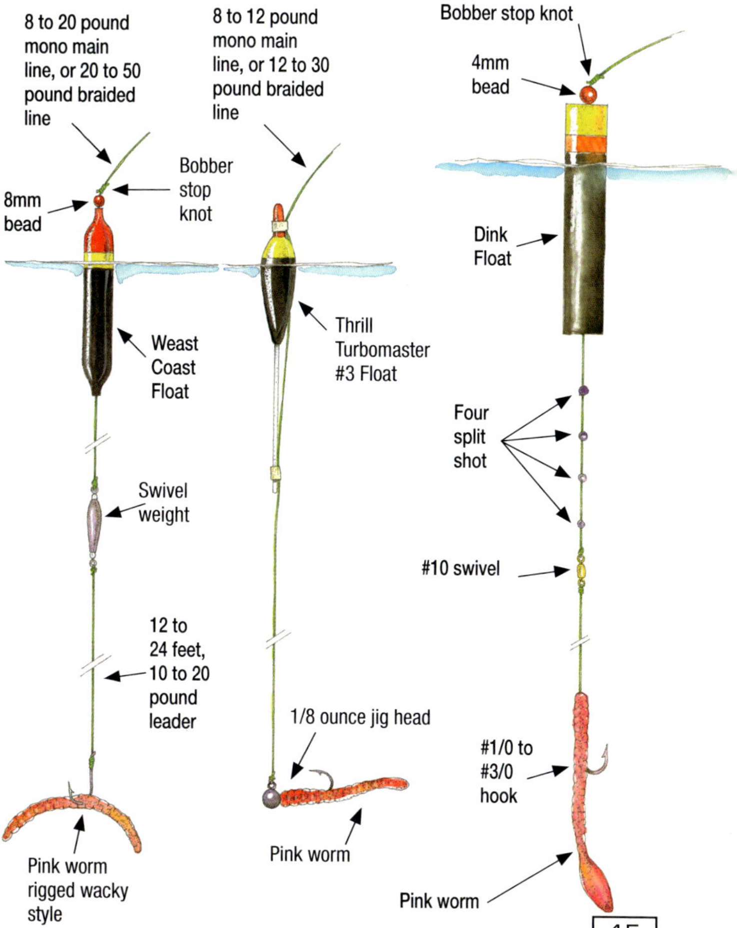

# SPAWN SAC RIG

**TIP**

You can make a Spawn Sac Rig by taking 10 or so salmon or trout eggs and creating a 'parcel' of eggs using any 'wedding vail' type material and then fishing it under a float or bottom drift rig.

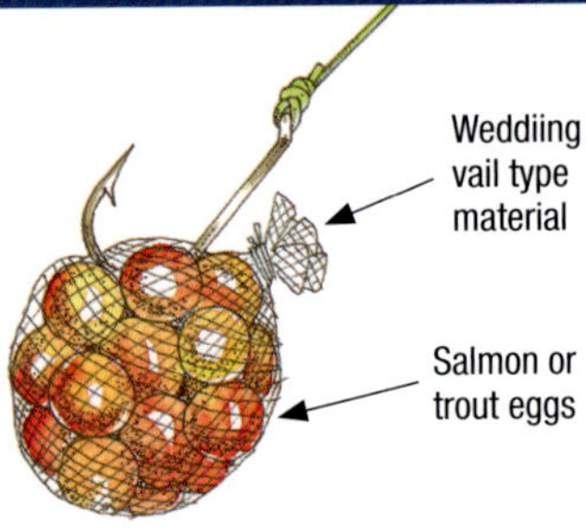


# DIVER AND BAIT RIGS

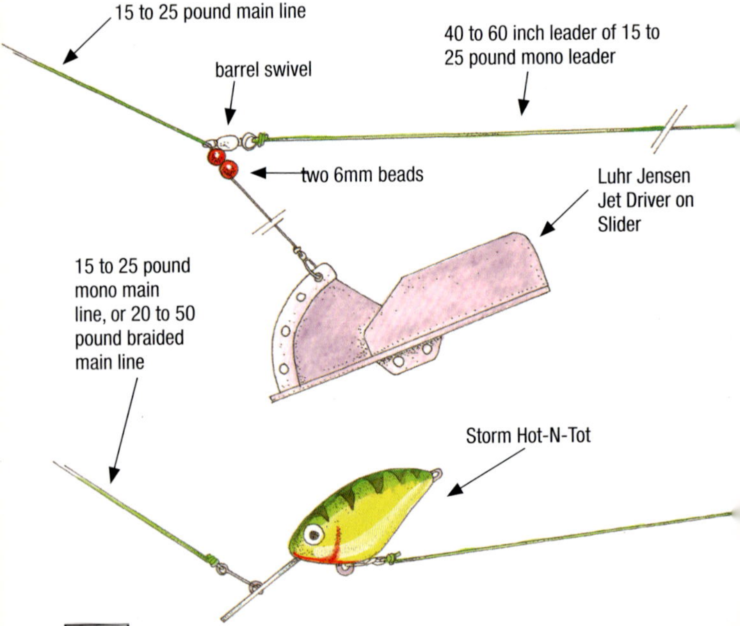

# PINK PLASTIC WORM RIG

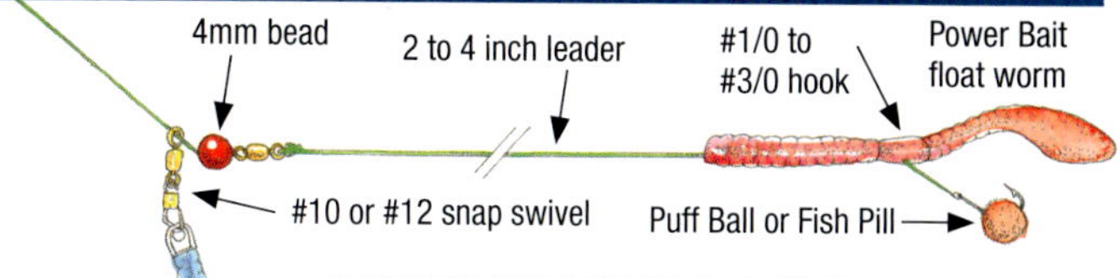


## TIP

Steelhead love plastic worms, and one of the best snag resistant rigs is a slinky sinker setup with a 4-6 inch worm. You can also run the worm upside down or 'half wacky' style to give the rig more action and fish pulling power.

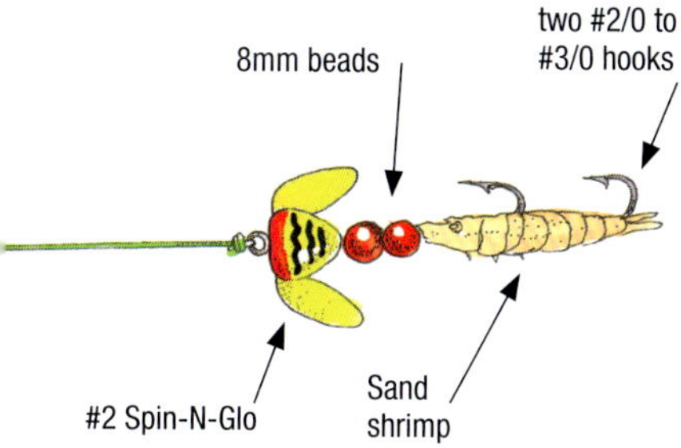


## TIP

There are a number of Diver and Bait Rigs that are suitable for targeting Steelhead. The two rigs shown are popular, but you can also rig pink worms etc and mix and match your divers and baits. Pulling a plastic worm behind a diver is a great way to catch steelhead

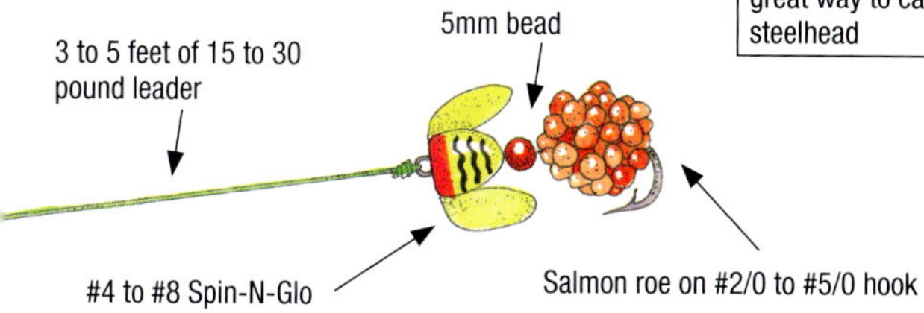

# SIDE-PLANER RIGS

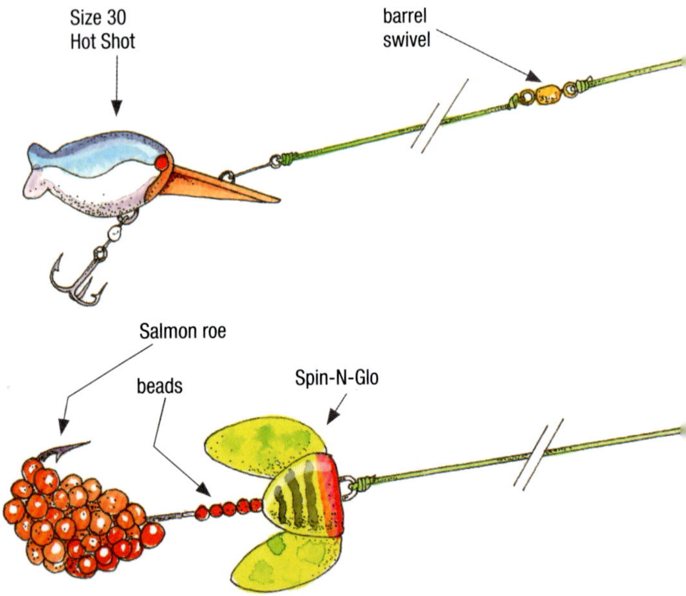


**TIP**

You don't need to have a boat to access midstream steelhead. While boat anglers are able to back-troll for steelhead by drifting back and forth across a river and dragging the lure through the schools of fish, shore anglers can utilize a side-planer to cover fish holding well out in the river and away from the bank.

The side-planer floats and has a rudder that swims the planer and lure away from the shore using the streams current, enabling the shore angler to target fish that can't be reached without a boat.

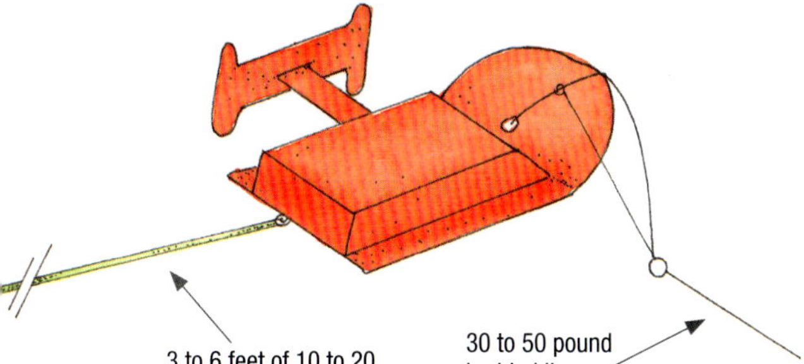


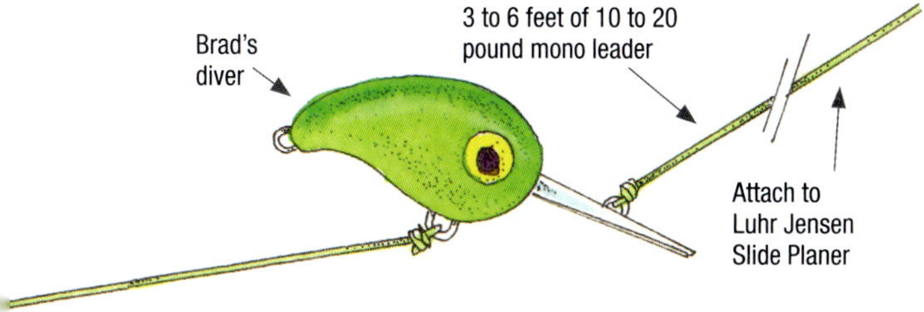


## STEELHEAD

Fresh run fish are super strong and offer one of the best fights of all the salmonoids. Because of the fish size and strength, top quality tackle is needed when targeting steelies. Fly anglers need to make long casts using big, bright flashy streamer or egg flies. Lure anglers use a variety of flashy spinners and spoons, again with bright colors in their makeup to elicit an aggressive hit. Salmon egg baits are usually used to entice these spawn run fish.

# RIGS

## Trout and Kokanee Rigs

### TROLLING RIG

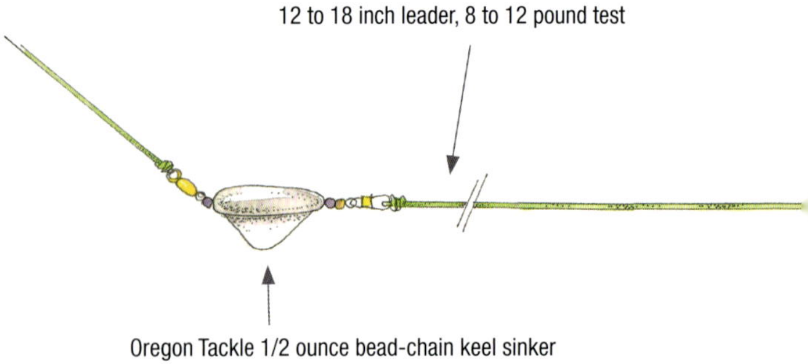

# BOTTOM RIG

**TIP**

Power baits are fantastic for fishing up off the bottom and above the weed. Any cruising trout, especially rainbows find it hard to resist a brightly colored artificial bait. These baits can also be used on dropper rigs when fishing a tight line back to the rod.

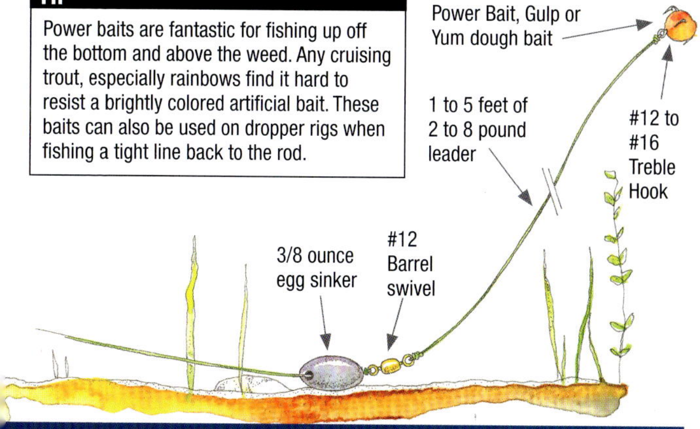


**TIP**

While flyfishing for Kokanee cruising shorelines can be successful in spring. By far the most productive method is by trolling the open water. Trolling very slowly while using your boats electronics to locate schools of fish is generally successful. Using dodgers and flashers to attract both Kokanee and trout is successful.

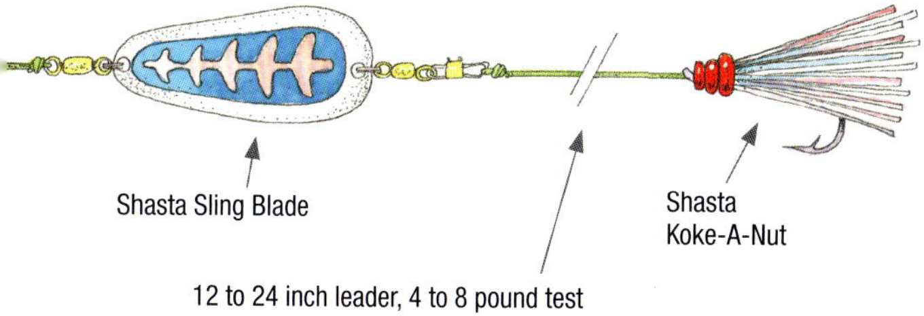

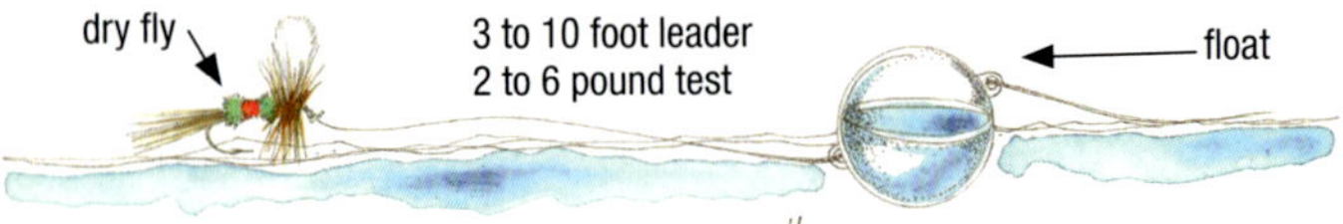


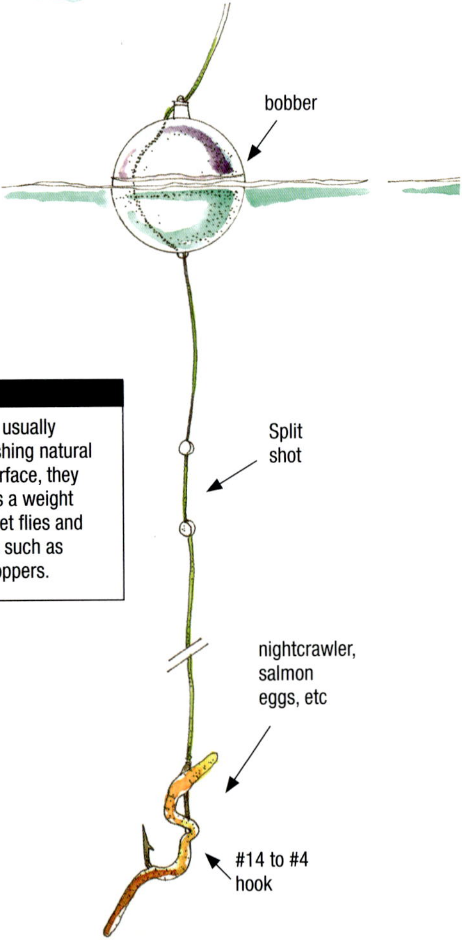


## TIP

While bobbers are usually associated with fishing natural baits below the surface, they can be effective as a weight to cast dry flies, wet flies and even surface baits such as crickets & grasshoppers.

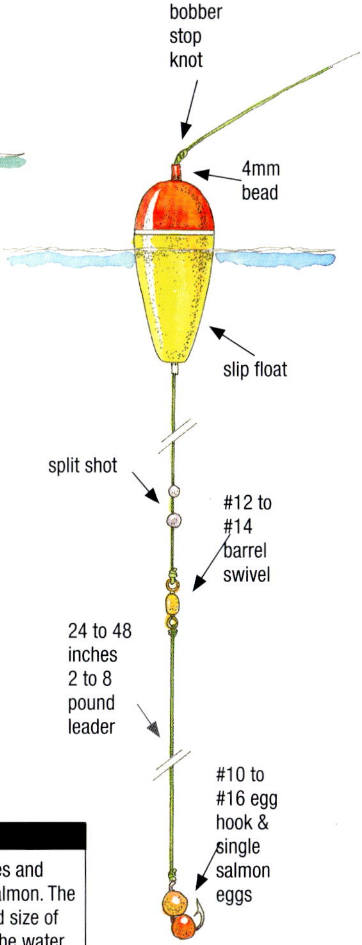


**TIP**

There are many different bobber styles and baits that are suitable for trout and salmon. The size of the bobbers, weight of line and size of hooks will usually be determined by the water conditions, size and type of fish your targeting and the size of the bait being used.

# DOWN RIGGER SETUPS

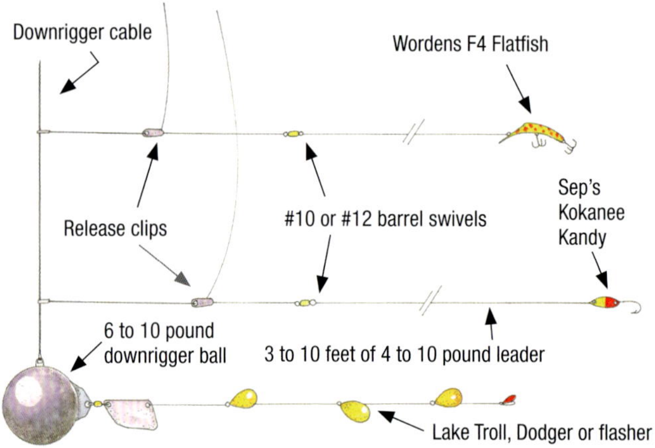


## TIP

Troll in "S" patterns with your boat rather than a straight line, this allows the lure to speed up and slow down which is enticing to trout and salmon. Troll at around 1.5 mph and use you electronics to locate the depth at which the fish are holding and employ downriggers to get the various rigs down to that depth.

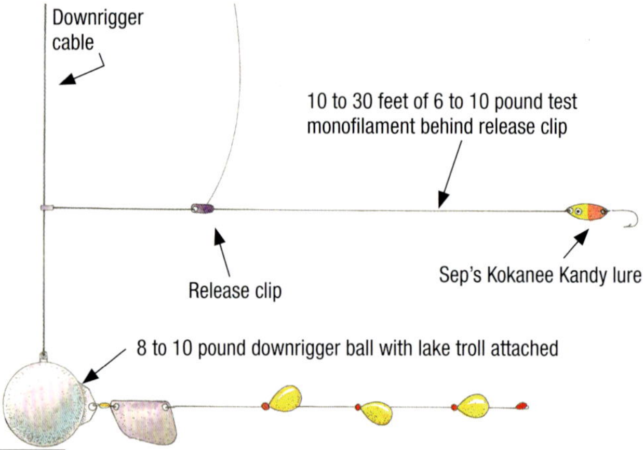

## BULL TROUT

A solid but not overly flashy fighter. Most fish are taken deep in lakes using strong baitcasting or spincasting tackle. Trolling deep with downriggers and lead lines.
They will eat live or dead baitfish, cut baits, spoons, diving plugs and streamer flies, all fished very deep for the most part.

## KOKANEE (LANDLOCKED SOCKEYE SALMON)

Their small size dictates the use of ultra light tackle. They have soft mouths so rods should be soft in action. They put up a good tussle on such gear. Despite being plankton feeders, they will hit small flashy spinners or spoons tipped with small pieces of worm. Anglers trolling strings of dodgers or blades ahead of these lures take most fish. Other anglers use baits including aquatic insects, corn, worms, salmon eggs fished on size 12-8 sized hooks.
Jigging with ¼ to 1 oz. jigs is effective when large schools are located.

## BROWN TROUT

Often given the title as the best freshwater sportfish in the world. They are strong, dogged fighters, often leaping in an effort to gain their freedom. They are almost the perfect sportfish, they will hit lures, flies and baits. Are renowned for being wary and not easily fooled. Trolling various spoons, plugs, spinners near the surface and down deep with downriggers is successful on lakes. Fishing dry flies, streamers and wet flies or lures and soft plastics in rivers and lakes are all productive.
Light spin cast and fly rods are generally used except when trolling big lures.
Will take natural baits such as live minnows, worms, crickets, grasshoppers & various aquatic food items.

## LAKE TROUT

A strong if not flashy fighting fish. An important sportfish. Most of the year fish are caught down deep using heavy spin or bait tackle and downriggers or lead lines. At these times the fish will take trolled spoons, diving plugs or live fish baits. In some areas, particularly in the far northern lakes, but in lower lakes during summer, fish will come in closer to shore and can then be targeted by anglers casting lures as well as flies.

## RAINBOW TROUT

A true sporting fish that runs hard and performs numerous leaps when hooked. A wide variety of tackle and rigs are suitable for chasing rainbow trout because of their vast range of habitats.
Spincasting, baitcasting and flyfishing are used, from ultralight outfits in mountain streams to stouter tackle in big rivers and lakes. Fish feed on the surface and down deep. Flyfishing with dry and wet flies, using floating and sinking lines in rivers and lakes, spincasting or trolling spoons, swimming and diving plugs, spinners.
Baitfishing using a variety natural and artificial baits such as worms, grasshoppers, minnows, corn kernels, marshmallows, artificial baits and salmon eggs.

# RIGGING Natural live baits

**LEARNING HOW TO RIG NATURAL BAITS SO THEY REMAIN ALIVE IS OFTEN THE KEY TO PUTTING MORE FISH IN THE BAG.**

## FROGS

### TIP

Frogs should be hooked lightly through the lip or either of the hind legs so that they can swim about naturally on the surface.

# CRICKETS AND GRASSHOPPERS

**TIP**

Hook lightly through the hard wing case area behind the head to allow the insects to kick about naturally.

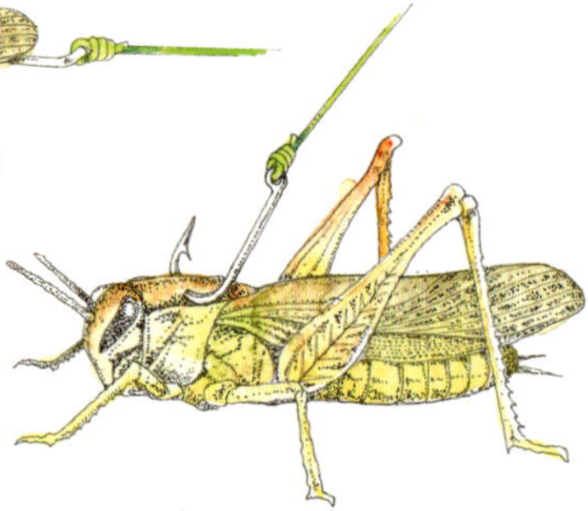

# CRAWDADS

**TIP**

Hook crawdads through the last segment near the tail and with the hook facing up and backwards so that it can move about without hooking up on the bottom.

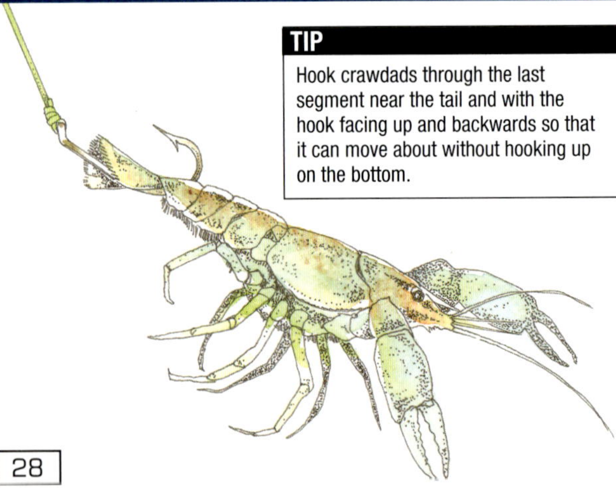

# NIGHTCRAWLERS

## TIP

There are a number of ways to rig nightcrawlers for fishing under a bobber, on the bottom or as retrieved live bait. Try and leave one or both ends free from the hook to encourage fish attracting movement.

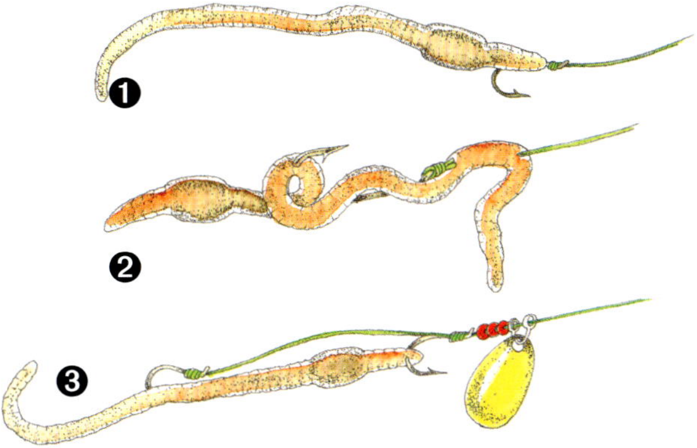


## TIP

❶ One of the most natural ways to rig nightcrawlers is to use a light line and small hook and allow the bait to drift naturally with the current flow through a pool. When fishing with this rig the fish will often pick it up as it drifts past in a very natural manner.

❷ The hook should be large enough to enable you to thread the worm onto the hook two or three times while allowing both ends of the worm to be free of the hook to swing about enticingly. Keep the hook size as small as possible to match the fish you're targeting also. If you're using smaller worms then load a few onto a hook so that fish such as catfish and carp have a good 'gob' of worms to eat.

❸ Attaching a spinner blade above a double hook rig can be very enticing to many fish. Rig some coloured beads above the first snelled hook to keep the spinner blade free of the first hook and attach the trail or stinger hook back from the tail of the nightcrawler to allow the tail to flutter about when being cast and retrieved, or trolled.

# CATERPILLARS AND SMALLER GRUBS

**TIP**

Caterpillars can be lightly hooked through the skin, while smaller, more delicate grubs can be attached to the hook with stretch thread. The key to fishing any small grubs is to use the appropriate hook size for the bait. Using chemically sharpened hooks also allows more hook ups. Caterpillars have tough skins so hooking directly through the back is the way to go, but when you're rigging delicate, small insects and grubs to very small hooks it often pays to use elasticized sewing thread to attach them to the hook rather than risk tearing the bait with the hook when rigging or casting.

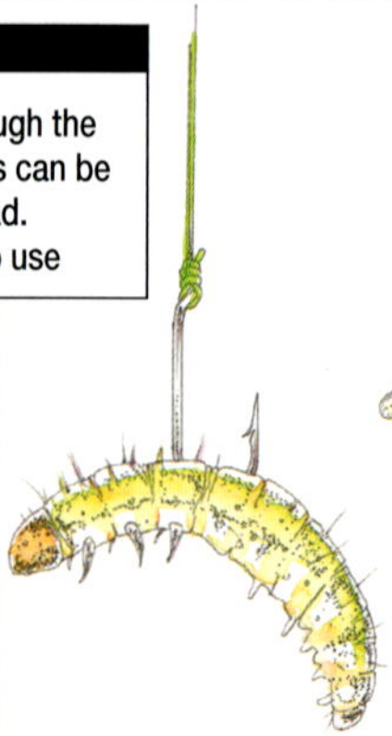

# MINNOWS

**TIP**

Minnows can be rigged on hooks with 'weed guards', or on small jig heads to fish amongst structure. Try rigging a spinner blade in front to increase the baits appeal from a distance when trolling.

## TIP

Live minnows and other baitfish are very versatile baits for any number of fish species. As with other natural baits it's preferable to rig them alive if possible to make them as attractive as possible to larger fish.
Fish baits including shiners, chubs, bluegill, pumpkinseed and sunfish are all contenders to be live rigged just so long as they can be legally used in the state or territory you're fishing in.

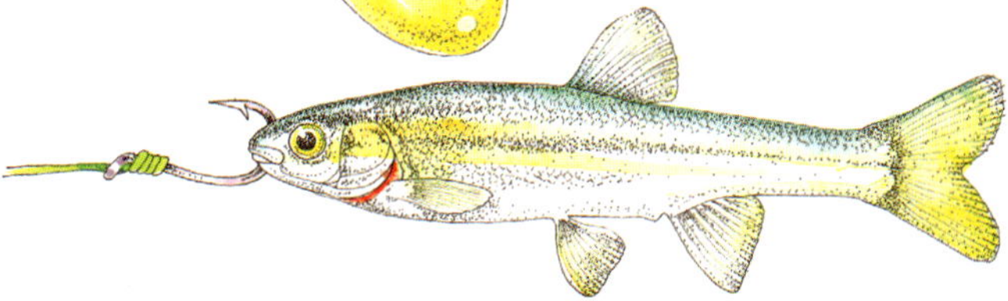

## TIP

The rigging methods shown are the simplest. Hook the minnow lightly (avoid piercing the backbone) through skin behind the dorsal fin so it tries to swim down deeper in the water column, or through the front lips to keep it swimming horizontal.

## TIP

When hooking live baitfish you can also hook through the back of the fish directly in front of the dorsal fin, this will make the baitfish swim higher in the water column. When you're chasing toothier fish such as pike and pickerel you can also use a treble hook instead of a single hook, although single hooks often provide the best hook up rates.

# NOTES